Anonymous

A summary of the vital statistics of the New England states

for the year 1892:

Being a concise statement of the marriages, divorces, births, and deaths in

the six New England states

Anonymous

A summary of the vital statistics of the New England states for the year 1892:
Being a concise statement of the marriages, divorces, births, and deaths in the six New England states

ISBN/EAN: 9783337763732

Printed in Europe, USA, Canada, Australia, Japan

Cover: Foto ©ninafisch / pixelio.de

More available books at **www.hansebooks.com**

THE NEW ENGLAND STATES.

The small circles show the location of the sixty-seven cities and towns having populations of more than 10,000 in each by the U. S. Census of 1890.

The figures within the circles refer to the first column in the table of cities and towns near the close of the book.

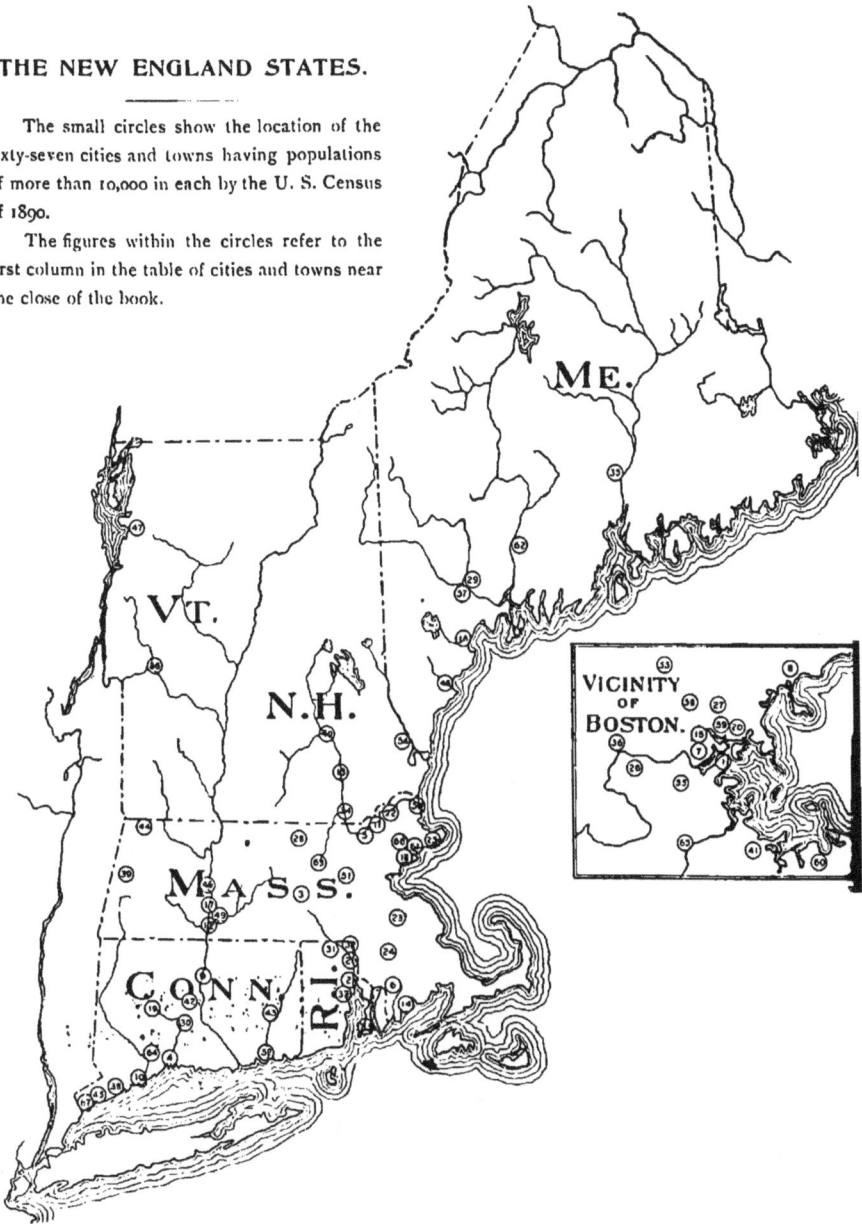

A SUMMARY

OF THE

VITAL STATISTICS

OF THE NEW ENGLAND STATES

FOR THE YEAR 1892.

BEING A CONCISE STATEMENT OF THE

MARRIAGES, DIVORCES, BIRTHS, AND DEATHS

IN THE SIX NEW ENGLAND STATES.

COMPILED UNDER THE DIRECTION OF THE SECRETARIES OF THE
STATE BOARDS OF HEALTH OF MAINE, NEW HAMPSHIRE,
VERMONT, MASSACHUSETTS, RHODE
ISLAND AND CONNECTICUT.

BOSTON:
DAMRELL & UPHAM, (the Old Corner Book Store).
LONDON:
P. S. KING & SON, 12 King St., Westminster.

INTRODUCTORY.

The object intended in publishing this summary, is to present in a condensed form, the Vital Statistics of the New England States as a whole. At any time previous to 1894 the publication of such a summary would have been impossible, in consequence of the fact that no compilation of the Vital Statistics of Maine was made until 1894, when the First Registration Report of that state for the year 1892 was issued.

At a meeting of the Secretaries of the Boards of Health of the six New England States, held in Montreal, in September, 1894, during the session of the American Public Health Association, it was decided to publish a summary of the Vital Statistics of these states. The objects to be secured by such a publication may be stated briefly as follows : —

1. The securing of better and more uniform methods of the presentation of material collected in the Registration Returns.

2. The stimulation of attention to this important branch of public work in other states, where registration has hitherto been neglected.

In New England the importance of registration of Vital Statistics has been acknowledged from the earliest periods of the existence of the colonies, a law having been enacted in 1639, in the Massachusetts Colony, providing for the keeping of a record "of every marriage, birth, and death of every person within the jurisdiction". This was followed soon afterward (1644) by similar legislation in Connecticut.

It was not until 1842 that any published report embracing these facts was made.

The six New England States have now published such reports for the stated periods as follows : —

Maine, . .	beginning with	1892
New Hampshire, .	"	"	1880
Vermont, .	"	"	1857
Massachusetts,	"	"	1842
Rhode Island,	"	"	1853
Connecticut,	"	"	1848

The importance of the subject of Vital Statistics as the basis or ground work of Public Hygiene is universally acknowledged, and the intimate connection of the one with the other is shown by the action of nearly every state government in uniting the Department of Registration of Vital Statistics with that of Public Health.

An unusual stimulus has been given to the progress of such work by the organization of general societies for the study and publication of statistics, of which the Royal Statistical Society of Great Britain, the International Statistical Institute, and the American Statistical Society are among the flourishing examples.

It is proposed to issue this summary at intervals of about five years, the second issue to embrace the statistics for 1895, since, in a portion of New England (two states embracing half the population) an intermediate census is taken, once in five years.

No account is taken in this summary, of the county as a division of the population, since this grouping or division has but little significance in New England, aside from its importance in connection with the administration of the courts of justice, the inquest laws, the control of highways and a few minor matters. The administration of the municipal affairs of the town or city, considered as a unit is a matter of far greater sanitary importance than that of the county. That the thorough and careful administration of such affairs, in such important matters as the introduction of pure water supplies, and efficient sewerage systems, the management and control of infectious diseases, the supervision of public institutions, the inspection of food, etc., has a perceptible effect upon the vital statistics of municipalities has been fully demonstrated, both in Europe and America, and we may add, in the distant cities of British India. For this reason the vital statistics of the principal towns are presented as fully as the limits of a summary of this character will admit.

A. G. YOUNG,
Secy. State Board of Health and Registrar Vital Statistics, Maine.

I. A. WATSON,
Secy. State Board of Health and Registrar of Vital Statistics, N. H.

J. H. HAMILTON,
Secy. State Board of Health, Vt.

SAML. W. ABBOTT,
Secret'y State Board of Health of Massachusetts.

G. T. SWARTS,
Secy. State Board of Health and Registrar of Vital Statistics, R. I.

C. A. LINDSLEY,
Secy. State Board of Health and Superintendent of Registration of Vital Statistics, Conn.

A SUMMARY OF THE VITAL STATISTICS OF THE NEW ENGLAND STATES.

POPULATION.

" Population is the basis of Vital Statistics, and hence demands preliminary consideration in any work bearing upon this subject." (Dr. Farr.)

The statements of population in this summary are those of the United States Census of 1880 and 1890, together with estimates made for the intercensal years, and for the years 1891 and 1892. The method of estimating is that which is employed in the annual reports of the Registrar General of England (the geometric rate of increase). Since short census intervals are preferable to long ones, the five year period is adopted for estimating, in those states where a quinquennial census is made. (Massachusetts and Rhode Island.)

In populations having a rapid growth, the results obtained by the arithmetric and geometric methods of estimating differ considerably, but in small communities, and especially among those of slow growth the difference is only slight, and scarcely affects the ratios representing the marriage, birth, and death rates to an appreciable degree. Hence, in estimating populations the geometric rate in this summary is only applied to the States, and in the table of cities and towns, to those cities which have a population larger than 20,000.

The population of the six states is shown in table I, by which it appears that the total population of the district in 1870 was 3,487,924 (U. S. Census), and this had increased to 4,010,529 in 1880, and 4,700,745 in 1890.

TABLE I.

Population of the New England States, 1880—1892.

	MAINE.	NEW HAMPSHIRE.	VERMONT.	MASSACHU- SETTS.	RHODE ISLAND.	CONNECTICUT.	NEW ENGLAND.
1870....	**626,915**	**318,300**	**330,551**	**1,457,351**	**217,353**	**537,454**	**3,487,924**
1880....	**648,936**	**346,991**	**332,286**	**1,783,085**	**276,531**	**622,700**	**4,010,529**
1881....	650,141	349,836	332,290	1,813,818	281,862	634,075	4,062,031
1882	651,348	352,708	332,312	1,845,081	287,290	645,058	4,114,401
1883....	652,557	355,600	332,326	1,876,883	292,834	657,452	4,107,652
1884....	653,768	358,517	332,340	1,909,233	298,529	669,452	4,221,839
1885....	654,981	361,458	332,354	**1,942,141**	**304,284**	681,081	4,276,899
1886....	656,197	364,423	332,367	1,998,174	312,114	694,133	4,357,408
1887....	657,416	367,413	332,380	2,053,823	320,145	706,813	4,439,090
1888....	658,637	370,427	332,394	2,115,136	328,388	719,724	4,524,706
1889....	659,860	373,466	332,408	2,176,159	336,843	732,871	4,611,607
1890....	**661,086**	**376,530**	**332,422**	**2,238,943**	**345,506**	**746,258**	**4,700,745**
1891....	662,314	379,618	332,436	2,303,536	354,396	759,890	4,792,190
1892....	663,544	382,932	332,450	2,369,983	363,515	773,971	4,886,405

Figures in **full-face** type are official census enumerations, all others are estimates.

The sum of the estimated populations for 1892 was 4,886,405.

The percentages which the population of each state bore to the total population of New England at each of the census enumerations of 1870, 1880 and 1890 were as follows:

PERCENTAGES OF TOTAL POPULATION.

STATES.	1870.	1880.	1890.
Maine,	17.97	16.18	14.06
New Hampshire,	9.13	8.65	8.01
Vermont,	9.48	8.28	7.07
Massachusetts,	41.78	44 46	47.63
Rhode Island,	6.23	6.90	7.35
Connecticut,	15.41	15.53	15 88
New England,	100.00	100.00	100.00

The annual rate of growth of each state (geometric) and that of the total population for the period 1880–1890 are expressed by the following figures:

Maine,	.0018+	Massachusetts,	.0230+
New Hampshire,	.0082+	Rhode Island,	.0225+
Vermont,	.00004	Connecticut,	.0183—

New England, .0160+

The rates of growth of Massachusetts and Rhode Island for the short intercensal period 1885–1890 were respectively .0288+ and .0257+.

Sex.

The ratios of the sexes in the different states at the two census enumerations (1880 and 1890) are shown in table 2, wherein it appears that the number of females was greater than that of the males in the whole district at each census, the exceptions being Vermont in each census and Maine in 1890. The most uniform distribution was in Maine in 1880 (1000 males to 1003 females), and the greatest excess of females was found in Rhode Island in 1880 (1000 males to 1079 females).

In England and Wales the ratio of males to females at the last census (1891) was as 1000 to 1063.

TABLE II.

Distribution of the Population by Sexes. Census of 1880 and 1890, with ratio of Females to 1,000 males, in each State.

	1880.				1890.			
	MALES.	FEMALES.	Females to 1,000 Males.	TOTAL.	MALES.	FEMALES.	Females to 1,000 Males.	TOTAL.
Maine........	324,058	324,578	1,003	648,636	332,500	328,496	987	661,086
New Hampshire..	170,526	176,465	1,035	346,991	186,566	189,964	1,018	376,530
Vermont.........	166,887	165,399	991	332,286	169,327	163,095	963	332,422
Massachusetts.....	858,440	924,645	1,077	1,783,085	1,087,700	1,151,234	1,058	2,238,943
Rhode Island......	133,030	143,501	1,079	276,531	168,025	177,481	1,056	345,506
Connecticut........	305,782	316,91	1 .6	622,700	369,538	376,720	1,020	746,258
New England......	1,958,723	2,051,896	1,048	4,010,529	2,313,755	2,386,990	1,032	4,700,745

Density of the Population.

Density of the population usually bears quite a definite relation to the condition of the people, and especially manifests its influence in the death rate. The population of New England exhibits extreme variations of density, from the sparsely settled Aroostook region of Maine to the densely populated wards of the large cities.

In table III. is presented the density of New England as a whole, and separately by states. The extremes of density were 21.7 persons per square mile in Maine, and 254.9 per square mile in Rhode Island in 1880, and 22.1 per square mile in Maine and 318.4 in Rhode Island in 1890.

The mean density of the whole district (New England) had increased from 64.7 per square mile in 1880 to 75.8 in 1890.

In the foregoing estimates, water surfaces amounting to 4460 square miles or 6.7 per cent. of the total area are excluded, leaving a land area of 62,005 square miles.

TABLE III.

Density of the Population.   Census of 1880 and 1890.

	Area in Square miles.	Population in 1880.	Persons to Square mile 1880.	Population in 1890.	Persons to Square mile. 1890.
Maine	29,895	648,936	21.7	661,086	22.1
New Hampshire..	9,005	346,991	38.5	376,530	41.8
Vermont.........	9,135	332,286	36.4	332.422	36.4
Massachusetts	8,040	1,783,085	221.8	2,238,943	278.5
Rhode Island.....	1,085	276,531	254.9	345,506	318.4
Connecticut......	4,845	622,700	128.5	746,258	154.0
New England...	62,005	4,010,529	64.7	4,700,745	75.8

Total area 66,465 miles, of which 4,460 or 6.7 per cent is water.

INTERNATIONAL VITAL STATISTICS.

The value of statistics is greatly enhanced by comparison, not only of the statistics of one state with those of neighboring states, but also with those of large populations embracing entire countries.

The usefulness of the well-arranged tables published in the preliminary portion of the Registrar General's Reports of England is everywhere acknowledged. In table IV the marriage, birth and death rates of the New England States are presented for a period of twenty years, and for the years 1891 and 1892. By this table it appears that the marriage rate of New England, as a whole, for the year 1892 (18.5 per 1000) was greater than that of any of the Transatlantic countries quoted in the table, the highest of any of these countries being that of Hungary (18.4) and the lowest, that of Ireland (9.3).*

The birth rate of New England in 1892 (24.9 per 1000 of the population) was less than those of any of the other countries except France and Ireland. Hungary had a birth rate of 40.3 and France 22 1.

The death rate of New England in 1892 (19.9) was less than those of Italy, Hungary, Austria, Germany, France, Holland and Belgium, and greater than those of the British Islands, Denmark, Norway, Sweden and Switzerland.

---

* NOTE.—In the previous year (1891) Hungary had a marriage rate of 17.2.

TABLE IV.

Summary of the Vital Statistics of the Principal Countries of Europe for Twenty Years, and for 1891 and 1892, together with those of the New England States.

STATES AND COUNTRIES	Twenty Years — 1871-1890				1891				1892			
	Marriage Rate	Birth Rate	Death Rate	Excess of Birth Rate over Death Rate	Marriage Rate	Birth Rate	Death Rate	Excess of Birth Rate over Death Rate	Marriage Rate	Birth Rate	Death Rate	Excess of Birth Rate over Death Rate
New England					18.5‖	25.2‖	19.0‖	5.3‖	18.5	24.9	19.9	5.0
Maine	18.6*	18.0*	18.0*		20.6	19.2*	18.7		17.3	20.7	18.4	2.3
New Hampshire	15.6	20.2	15.1	5.1	16.9	20.0	16.2	3.8	21.3	19.1	20.1	
Vermont	18.1	25.7	19.7	6.0	18.3	27.4	19.6	7.8	17.5	19.7	17.9	1.8
Massachusetts	18.7	23.7	18.0	5.7	18.7	25.8	18.7	7.1	19.0	27.8	20.6	7.2
Rhode Island	16.0	23.6	17.1	6.5	17.1	23.3	18.9	3.3	19.3	24.5	20.4	4.2
Connecticut									17.0	24.5	19.6	4.9
England and Wales	15.6	34.0	20.3	13.7	15.6	31.4	20.2	11.2	15.4	30.5	19.0	11.5
Scotland	13.9	33.6	20.4	13.2	13.9	31.2	20.7	10.5	14.1	30.7	18.5	12.2
Ireland	9.0	24.9	18.0	6.9	9.2	23.1	18.4	4.7	9.3	22.4	19.4	3.0
Italy	15.6	37.3	28.6	8.7	15.0	37.3	26.2	11.1	15.0	36.3	26.2	10.1
Denmark	15.2	31.7	19.0	12.7	13.6	31.0	20.0	11.0	13.6	29.5	19.4	10.1
Norway	13.7	30.7	16.9	13.8	13.2	30.9	17.5	13.4	12.6	29.6	17.7	11.9
Sweden	13.1	29.8	17.6	12.2	11.0	28.3	16.8	11.5	11.4	27.0	17.9	9.1
Austria	16.3	38.6	30.6	8.0	15.4	38.1	27.0	10.2	15.6	36.2	28.8	7.4
Hungary†	19.1	44.0	33.7	10.3	17.2	42.3	33.1	9.2	18.4	40.3	35.0	5.3
Switzerland	14.7	29.4	22.1	7.3	14.3	28.2	20.7	7.5	14.7	28.0	19.3	8.7
German Empire‡	16.4	38.1	26.0	12.1	16.1	37.0	23.4	13.0	15.9	35.7	24.1	11.6
Holland	15.1	35.2	22.6	12.6	14.2	33.7	20.7	13.0	14.4	32.0	21.0	11.0
Belgium	14.2	31.0	21.4	9.6	14.8	29.6	21.0	8.6	15.4	28.9	21.8	7.1
France	15.4	24.6	22.8	1.8	15.0	22.6	22.6	0.0	15.2	22.1	22.6	—0.5§

* Seven years. Registration of births said to be defective. † Fifteen years. ‡ Nineteen years. § Excess of death rate.

‖ Fifteen years. In the figures for New England for 1891 Maine is not included.

MARRIAGES.

The total number of marriages registered in New England in 1892 was 45,310, which, in an estimated population of 4,886,405, gives a marriage rate of 9.27, or, according to the more common method of reckoning, in which the ratio of persons married is employed, instead of the number of marriages, the rate was 18.54 per 1,000 of the population.

The highest marriage rate was in New Hampshire where it was 21.28 per 1,000, and the lowest, 17.04 was in Connecticut.

The following table presents the marriages and marriage rates for 1892 : —

TABLE V.

MARRIAGES AND MARRIAGE RATES OF THE NEW ENGLAND
STATES — 1892.

	Marriages 1892.	Marriage rate per 1,000 (population, 1892.	Marriage rates (persons married).	Marriage rate, 1891.
Maine,	5,726	8.63	17 26	——
New Hampshire,	4,074	10.64	21.28	20 56
Vermont,	2,905	8.74	17.48	16.94
Massachusetts,	22,507	9.50	19.00	18.82
Rhode Island,	3,502	9.63	19.26	18.74
Connecticut,	6,596	8.52	17.04	17.07
New England,	45,310	9 27	18.54	18 50

The foregoing marriage rates are generally higher than those of other countries having registration, as shown in table IV., p. 15.

Marriages by Months.

In table VI are presented the statistics of marriages by months in four of the states, Maine, New Hampshire, Massachusetts, and Rhode Island, by which it appears that the greatest number of marriages in any month in these states was celebrated in

TABLE VI.

MARRIAGES BY MONTHS—1892.

(Four States.)

	January.	February.	March.	April.	May.	June.	July.	August.	September.	October.	November.	December.	Unknown.	Total.
Maine	321 66.6	334 74.1	322 66.8	456 97.8	390 80.9	542 116.3	444 92.1	437 90.7	567 121.6	569 118.1	614 149.7	608 126.2	3	5,726
New Hampshire	285 83.4	303 94.8	257 69.4	313 94.6	390 87.8	409 123.6	268 78.4	278 81.3	396 120.0	441 125.0	445 131.6	390 105.3	39	4,074
Massachusetts	1,633 85.6	1,719 96.4	1,087 64.4	1,701 97.1	1,657 96.9	2,680 145.8	1,493 78.3	1,507 83.7	2,179 118.1	2,455 128.8	2,716 147.2	1,525 80.5	5	22,507
Rhode Island	275 92.7	289 104.2	180 60.7	268 93.4	250 87.4	429 149.5	218 73.5	246 83.0	320 111.6	408 137.6	382 133.1	228 76.9	—	3,502
Four States	2,514 83.1	2,645 93.4	1,776 58.7	2,828 96.6	2,606 86.1	4,070 139.0	2,423 80.0	2,558 84.4	3,462 118.2	3,873 123.0	4,241 144.8	2,731 90.3	32	35,800

The first line of figures for each State and for the four States represents the number of marriages in each month, and the second line of smaller figures shows the intensity of the marriage rate in each month, as compared with a monthly mean of 100. The effect of the unequal length of the months is eliminated.

the month of November, as well as for each one of these states, except Rhode Island, in which the greatest number occurred in June. The months having the next greatest number were December in Maine, October in New Hampshire and Rhode Island, and June in Massachusetts.

For these four states the month having the least number was March, and for the separate states, January in Maine, and March in each of the remaining states.

For the sake of comparison, these figures are reproduced according to the method employed in the Registrar General's Report of England (1892) by quarters of the year.

PERSONS MARRIED TO EACH 1,000 LIVING.

Quarter Ending.	England 55 years, 1838-1892.	England, 1892.	New England, 1892.
March,	13.2	11 7	14.7
June,	16.4	16.4	20.2
September,	15.6	15.7	17 9
December,	19.1	17.8	23.0
Mean of whole period,	16.1	15.4	18.5*

* This average refers to all New England: — for the four states embraced in this monthly table the average was 18.9.

In summing up this subject, in a recent work, Dr. Leffingwell says: " Religious and social customs intervene in most civilized countries, and create prejudices for or against the celebration of marriage during particular seasons of the year.

In France and Italy the majority of nuptials are in February. In Ireland, particularly in the west and south, more than half the Catholic marriages are celebrated between Christmas and Shrovetide. In Scotland there is a strong prejudice against marrying in May. Agricultural populations object to the season of harvest and defer such ceremonies till October and November. In Russia more than three-fourths of all marriages occur in autumn and winter."

" *Influence of seasons on Conduct.*"—LEFFINGWELL.

TABLE VII.

MARRIAGES BY AGES — 1892.

(Five States.)

	Under 20.		20-30.		30-40.		40-50.		50-60.		60-70.		70-80.		Over 80.		Age not stated.		Totals.
	M.	F.	M.	F.	M.	F.	M.	F.	M.	F.	M.	F.	M.	F.	M.	F.	M.	F.	
Maine.........	194	1,621	3,724	3,118	1,066	580	378	210	180	196	83	27	33	3	3	1	55	44	5,728
New Hampshire	184	1,109	2,652	2,241	743	450	253	154	133	70	72	27	24	3			31	20	4,074
Massachusetts ..	427	3,607	15,577	15,306	4,472	2,625	1,280	700	513	193	214	66	58	9	5		21	1	22,507
Rhode Island...	81	587	2,431	2,399	1,065	456	214	109	66	29	37	7	7				1	5	3,502
Connecticut	119	1,015	4,504	4,517	1,270	761	250	206	158	47	73	45	24	4	1	1			6,506
Five States......	1,005	7,939	28,978	27,491	8,616	4,872	2,440	1,385	1,051	435	489	172	146	19	9	1	71	91	42,405

Marriages by Ages — Table VII.

Of the whole number of men married in New England in 1892, whose ages were known, 97 per cent. were between the ages of 20 and 60 years.

Of the whole number of women, whose ages were known, 80.8 per cent. were between the ages of 20 and 60 years.

Sixty-eight and four tenths per cent. of the men and 64.9 per cent of the women were between the ages of 20 and 30 years

Early Marriages.

Two and four tenths per cent. of the men who were married, whose ages were known, and 18.8 per cent. of the women were under 20 years of age.

The highest per cent. of men married (4.5), who were under 20, was in New Hampshire, and the lowest (1.8) was in Connecticut.

The highest per cent. of females married under 20 (27.6) was in Maine, that of New Hampshire for the same class being nearly the same (27.3); and the lowest per cent of females married (of the same class, 15.4) was in Connecticut.

Late Marriages.

One and five tenths per cent. of the men marrried, whose ages were known, and less than five tenths of one per cent. of the women married were over 60 years of age.

The highest percentage of men married, who were more than 60 years of age, was 2.36 and was in New Hampshire; and the lowest percentage of the same class was in Massachusetts (1.23).

The highest ratio of females of this class who were married was seven tenths of one per cent. and this percentage prevailed both in New Hampshire and in Connecticut, and the lowest (two tenths of one per cent.) was in Rhode Island.

Marriages by Nativity — Table VIII.

Considerable importance, possibly an undue amount, has been attached to the term " nativity " as employed in American

TABLE VIII.

MARRIAGES BY NATIVITY—1892.

State.	Bride and Groom Native.	Bride and Groom Foreign.	Groom Native.	Bride Native.	Unknown	Total.	Percentages of Persons Married. Native.	Foreign.
Maine...............	3565	448	272	330	1121	5726	84.0	16.0
New Hampshire.......	2457	856	318	278	185	4074	70.3	29.7
Vermont............	*	*	*	*	12	2465*	85.9	14.1
Massachusetts.......	10,032	7647	2558	2289	1	22,507	55.3	44.7
Rhode Island........	1672	1100	343	387	–	3502	58.2	41.8
Connecticut........	3529	1988	532	576	1	6596	67.6	32.4
New England (Persons Married)........	Native 55,303	Foreign 32,67.			2440	90,620	62.9	37.1

* The statistics of Vermont upon this point are specified only with regard to the number of persons married of each class without reference to the number of marriages. There were 4970 persons married of native birth and 816 of foreign birth, and 24 in which the nativity was unknown.

The unknown are excluded in estimating the percentages in the last two columns.

Statistical Documents. It should be borne in mind, however, that nearly the entire population of New England is derived from races foreign to the soil. Those whose ancestry in this country dates back to the early history of the colonies count but nine or ten generations at the longest.

The term " nativity ", therefore, conveys but little meaning, when applied to percentages comprising portions of the population, since it has reference to the persons of a single generation, without regard to their parentage or ancestry, immediate or remote. The term "parent-nativity" embraces only one more generation, while there are no statistics which include generations earlier than the parents.

In the statistics of marriages on page 21 the term " nativity " is employed with reference only to the persons married and has no relation to their parentage.

The statistics embraced in this table show that the total number of marriages in New England in 1892 was 45,310, or 90,620 persons. Of this number, the nativity of 2640 was unspecified; 55,303 were natives, or 62.9 per cent. of those whose nativity was specified; and 32,677, or 37.1 were of foreign birth.

The percentages in the last two columns of table VIII. show that the highest ratio of persons of native birth married in 1892 was in Vermont, and the least in Massachusetts.

DIVORCES.

This portion of the summary will necessarily be less complete in detail than those portions which relate to vital statistics, properly so-called, in consequence of a greater want of uniformity in the methods of collection of the returns of divorces in the different states.

Divorce statistics were not introduced into the Registration Reports of any of the States until a comparatively recent period, but they now form a part of these reports in each one of the New England States.

The whole number of divorces granted in New England in

1892 was 2,653, and these were distributed as follows. The numbers for 1891 are also presented, except those of Maine:

	1892.	1891.		1892.	1891.
Maine	552	*	Massachusetts	790	799
New Hampshire	347	412	Rhode Island	296	275
Vermont	167	165	Connecticut	501	475
			Totals	2,653	2,126

Relative Distribution.

In the following table Column 1 presents the number of divorces granted in each 10,000 of the population in 1892. Column 2 presents the number granted as compared with each 100 marriages in 1892; and the same ratios for 1891 are given in Column 3:

Divorces in New England — Relative Distribution.

STATES.	1 Number in each 10,000 of population. 1892.	2 Number in 100 marriages. 1892.	3 Number in 100 marriages. 1891.
Maine	8.3	9.6	. . .
New Hampshire	9.0+	8.5	10.5
Vermont	5.0	5.7	5.9
Massachusetts	3.3	3.5	3.7
Rhode Island	8.1	8.4	8.3
Connecticut	6.5	7.6	7.3
New England	5.4	5.8	5.6

By this table it appears that the highest number granted in 1892 as compared with the population was in New Hampshire (9.05 per 10,000), and the lowest was in Massachusetts (3.3.)

As compared with the number of marriages the highest percentage in 1892 was in Maine (9.6), and the lowest percentage was in Massachusetts (3 5.)

Sex of Libellants in Cases where Divorces were Granted.

This is presented in four states only, — Maine, New Hampshire, Vermont and Massachusetts.

The figures are as follows : —

STATES.	Men.	Women.	Total.	Ratio of men to 100 women.
Maine	142	410	552	35
New Hampshire . .	103	244	347	42
Vermont . .	53	114	167	46
Massachusetts	246	544	790	45
Total .	544	1,312	1,856	41

The mean ratio of male to female libellants was 41 to 100. The greatest difference in the numbers of the sexes of libellants was in Maine (35 men to 100 women), and the least difference was in Vermont (46 men to 100 women.)

Legal Causes of Divorce.

The following table presents the statutory causes for which divorces may be granted in the New England states. Some of these causes are very rarely presented for the purpose of obtaining divorce : —

Causes for which Divorces may be granted in the New England States.

The following are the principal causes for which divorces may be granted in the New England States : —

Maine.—Adultery ; extreme cruelty ; impotence ; utter desertion for three years next prior to filing of libel ; gross and confirmed habits of intoxication ; cruel and abusive treatment ; gross or wanton neglect or refusal to provide maintenance for wife ; nullity of marriage.

New Hampshire. — Divorce may be granted to either party for adultery ; impotence ; extreme cruelty ; conviction of crime punishable by imprisonment for more than one year and actual imprisonment; treatment injurious to health, treatment to endanger reason; absence for three years together and not heard from; habitual drunkenness for three years; joining a religious sect which professes to believe the relation of husband and wife unlawful; refusal to cohabit; abandonment for three years; nullity of marriage; also to the wife if husband has been willingly absent for three years without making provision for support of wife; to the husband, if wife has willingly absented herself for three years; if wife has gone out of state and remained away for three years; to the wife, if wife of an alien has lived in New Hampshire for three years, and husband has left the United States to become a citizen of some foreign country and has not returned.

Vermont. To either party for adultery; imprisonment for life, intolerable severity; wilful desertion for three years, or for seven years, and not heard from.

To wife, if husband, being able, grossly or wantonly and cruelly neglects to maintain her.

Massachusetts. To either party for adultery; impotence; extreme cruelty; utter desertion for three consecutive years next prior to filing of the libel; gross and confirmed habits of intoxication; cruel and abusive treatment.

To the wife, when the husband, being sufficiently able, grossly or wantonly refuses or neglects to provide suitable maintenance for her.

Also, when either party has separated from the other without his or her consent, and has united with a religious sect or society that professes to believe the relation of husband and wife void or unlawful, and has so continued for three years, and meantime refuses to cohabit.

Or when either party has been sentenced to imprisonment at hard labor for life, or for five years or more. Gross and confirmed drunkenness from opium and other drugs.

Rhode Island. To either party for adultery; impotence; extreme cruelty; wilful desertion for five years; or for a shorter time in the discretion of the court; continued drunkenness;

when either party is deemed to be (on account of punishment for crime), civilly'dead, or is presumed to be naturally dead, for other gross misbehevior, or wickedness of either party.

To the wife, for neglect or refusal, on the part of husband, being able, to provide for her.

Connecticut Adultery ; fraudulent contract; wilful desertion for three years with total neglect of duty ; seven years' absence ; during which period the absent party has not been heard from ; habitual intemperance ; intolerable cruelty ; sentence to imprisonment for life; any infamous crime involving a violation of conjugal duty.

In the following table are presented the statistics of divorces granted in New England by causes for the year 1892, for the states of Maine, New Hampshire, Vermont, Massachusetts and Connecticut.

CAUSES OF DIVORCE, 1892.

Causes.	Maine.	N. H.	Vt.	Mass.	Conn.	Total.	Per-ce't'ge.
Adultery	70	75	27	166	82	420	17.8
Desertion	181	143*	78*	376	219	997	42.5
Intoxication or habitual drunkenness . .	82	22	—	104	105	313	13.3
Cruel and abusive treatment	115	—	—	86	—	201	8 5
Extreme cruelty . .	—	89	42	18	69	218	9.2
Neglect to provide for wife	17	—	11	29	—	57	2.4
Imprisonment . . .	—	2	1	4	—	7	.3
Nullity of marriage .	4	2	—	6	—	12	.5
All other causes* . .	83	14	8	1	26	132*	5.5
	522	347	167	790	501	2,357	100.0

NOTE. New Hampshire.— These 143 cases included in the title "Desertion" include 14 classed as granted "for three years' absence." Vermont.—Seventy-eight divorces for "desertion and wilful desertion ;" 42 divorces for "intolerable severity. The title, "All other causes," embraces several divorces in which a combination of causes was alleged in the application.

Marriages of the Divorced.

The following additional information is contained in the reports of New Hampshire, Rhode Island and Connecticut:—

MARRIAGES OF THE DIVORCED, 1892.

	Men.	Women.	Total.
New Hampshire	86	90	176
Rhode Island .	59	78	137
Connecticut .	151	159	310
	296	327	623

BIRTHS.

In accordance with common practice, the term births in this summary means *living births.* Still-births are, therefore, considered in a separate category, since they form no addition to the living population. Likewise, as deaths they subtract nothing from the living population; hence they are not included in the death-rate.

The term birth-rate also means the ratio of children born alive to the living population for the same reason.

The number of births registered in New England in 1892 was 121,353, and the birth-rate was 24.8.*

The highest birth-rate was in Massachusetts (27.8) and the lowest (19.1) was that of New Hampshire.*

*NOTE—It is probable that in the two states, Maine and New Hampshire, in which Registration has been operative for a shorter time than it has in the four other states, the registration of births is considerably defective. For example, the registered births in the thriving manufacturing cities of Manchester, Dover, Portsmouth, Portland and Auburn, having a population of over 114,000 in 1890, were only 2,445 in 1892, while the deaths in the same year were 2,543. Making due allowance for growth of population these indicated a birth-rate of about 20.5 and a death-rate of about 21.5. A population of this character should have had a birth-rate of not less than 27 per 1000, and there was probably a deficiency in registration of not less than 800 births in these cities. Making due allowance for increase of population there was probably a deficiency of about 3,300 births in Maine and 2,000 births in New Hampshire. The addition of these numbers would raise the birth-rate of Maine to 23.4 and that of New Hampshire to 25.1 and the combined birth-rate of New England to 25.9.

TABLE IX.

Births — 1892.

STATES.	Whole Number.	SEX.			PARENTAGE.					PLURAL BIRTHS.				ILLEGITIMATE.				STILL BIRTHS.			
		Male.	Female.	Unknown.	Both Native.	Both Foreign.	Native Mother.	Native Father.	Not stated.	Total.	Male.	Female.	Unknown.	Total.	Male.	Female.	Unknown.	Total.	Male.	Female.	Unknown.
Maine............	13,758	7,038	6,634	86	8,089	2,590	883	945	921	276	131	139	6	......	......	......	......	270	146	96	28
New Hampshire..	7,327	3,688	3,576	63	3,646	2,727	564	541	268	†170	100	78	1	......	......	......	......	419	217	164	38
Vermont.........	6,558	3,365	3,187	6	*	*	*	*	*	124	70	54	......	71	17	54	......	237	122	99	16
Massachusetts ..	65,824	33,758	31,951	115	21,800	29,895	6,767	6,019	443	†1168	579	589	......	990	507	472	11	2,293	1,370	845	78
Rhode Island...	8,899	4,548	4,351	......	2,056	4,192	876	875	......	168	92	76	......	95	42	53	......	371	217	154	......
Connecticut	18,987	9,653	9,220	114	7,800	7,000	1,079	1,441	377	1401	205	195	1	106	111	85	......	763	456	298	9
	121,353	62,050	58,019	384	......	......	......	......	......	2,316	1,177	1,131	8	......	......	......	......	4,353	2,528	1,656	103

* The figures for Vermont are given without reference to "mixed" parentage, and are stated as follows: American, 5,090; Foreign, 1,423; Unknown, 45.
† Includes one case of triplets in New Hampshire, eight cases in Massachusetts, and one case in Connecticut, the remainder being twins.

The following table presents the births and birth-rates in New
England in 1892:

BIRTHS AND BIRTH—RATES IN NEW ENGLAND IN 1892.

States.	Registered living births, 1892.	Birth-rates, 1892.	Birth-rates, 1891.
Maine	13,758	20.7	———
New Hampshire	7,327	19.1	19.2
Vermont . .	6,558	19 7	20.0
Massachusetts	65,824	27.8	27.4
Rhode Island	8,899	24.5—	25.8
Connecticut .	18,987	24.5+	23.5
	121,353	24.8	25 2

Births by Sexes—Table IX.

Of the whole number of living births, in which the sex was
known, 62,050 were boys and 58,919 were girls, being in the
ratio of 1,053 males to 1,000 females.   The ratios in the different states were as follows, to 1,000 females in each : Maine,
1,061 ; New Hampshire, 1,031 ; Vermont, 1,056 ; Massachusetts,
1,057 ; Rhode Island, 1,045 and Connecticut, 1,047.

In England, for the period of 54 years, 1838–'91, the ratio
was 1,043 males to 1,000 females, but the difference has
diminished with considerable uniformity from 1,052 in the five-
year period (1841–'45) to 1,036 in the period (1886–'90).

The proportion of male to female births in other foreign
countries was as follows for the ten-year period, 1870–'79:
(Newsholme.)

Males born to every 1000 females born :

Italy,	1,071	German Empire,	1,062
Austria,	1,068	Holland,	1,061
France,	1,064	Belgium,	1,059
Switzerland,	1,063	Scotland,	1,057
	Ireland,	1,056.	

Births—Parent Nativity.—Out of 113,484 registered births in
the states of Maine, New Hampshire, Massachusetts, Rhode

Island and Connecticut, 44,981 or 39.7 per cent. were of native parentage, 47,013 or 41.4 per cent. were of foreign parentage, and 21,490 were of mixed parentage (foreign father and native mother, or native father and foreign mother.)

[The returns of Rhode Island and Connecticut are not strictly comparable in this particular, with those of the other states, but the discrepancy (which cannot readily be eliminated) would only affect the result to a very slight degree.]

In the returns of Vermont, not included in the foregoing figures, no account is taken of births of mixed parentage, and the figures are as follows for births, the parentage of which was known: American, 5,090 or 78.2 per cent; foreign, 1,423 or 21.8 per cent.

The proportion of children born of native and of foreign parentage differed considerably in the different states, the figures being as follows:—

Parentage of Children Born Alive. — Percentages.

	Of Native Parentage.	Of Foreign Parentage.	Mixed Parentage.
Maine	66.3	19.8	13.9
New Hampshire . . .	48.8	36.5	14.7
Massachusetts . .	33.4	45.7	20.9
Rhode Island . . .	33.2	47.2	19.6
Connecticut .	42.4	40.9	16.7
New England . . .	39.7	41.4	18.9

No true estimate of the relative fecundity of the native and foreign-born population can be made from these figures since, as Dr. Newsholme shows, the two classes are not strictly comparable.

Still births — Table IX.—The total number of still-births registered in New England in 1892 was 4,353, being in the ratio of 35.9 per 1,000 of living births, that of 1891 being 34.8 for all of the states except Maine.

In the different states these ratios were as follows:—

Still Births, Ratio per 1000 *Living Births.*

	1892	1891		1892	1891
Maine,	19.6	—–	Massachusetts,	34.8	35.3
New Hampshire,	54.1	29.2	Rhode Island,	41.7	29.7
Vermont,	36.1	37.3	Connecticut,	40.2	37.0
New England				35.9	34.8

Of the whole number 2,528 were males and 1,656 were females, while the sex of 169 was not stated. The ratio of males to females was as 153 of the former to 100 of the latter. The least variation in sex was in Vermont, which had a ratio of 123 still-born males to 100 still-born females, and the greatest in Massachusetts, where the ratio was 162 to 100.

Similar variations are known to prevail elsewhere. Those of France, Italy, Belgium, Sweden and Russia being respectively, 144, 140, 135, 133 and 129 males to 100 females for the period 1865–1875.

Plural Births — *Table IX.* — The number of registered plural births in New England in 1892 was 1,153 and the product of such births was 2,316 children, of which number 2,286 were twins, and 30 were triplets.

This was equivalent to one twin birth in 106 cases. Of the whole number, 1,177 were boys, 1,131 were girls, and the sex of eight was unknown. The ratio of males to females differed but little from those of all births, being in the proportion of 1,041 males to 1,000 females.

Of the cases of triplets — one occurred in New Hampshire, one in Connecticut, and eight in Massachusetts.

Illegitimacy. — *Table IX.*

The facts in relation to illegitimate births are presented in the registration returns of four states — Vermont, Massachusetts, Rhode Island and Connecticut. In these states returns were made of 1,348 illegitimate births, which was in the ratio of 13.4 per 1,000 living births in these states.

The ratio in the different states was as follows : —

In Vermont, 10.2 per 1,000 births.
In Massachusetts, 15.0 per 1,000 births.
In Rhode Island, 10.7 per 1,000 births.
In Connecticut, 10.3 per 1,000 births.
Of the whole number, 660 were males and 610 were females.

Illegitimate Birth-Rates in Other Countries.

Countries.	Illegitimate births per 1,000 births.	Countries.	Illegitimate births per 1,000 births.
Ireland .	25	Norway . . .	82
Russia .	28	Scotland	84
Holland . .	30	German Empire .	89
Switzerland . . .	47	Denmark . . .	101
England and Wales	48	Sweden . . .	101
Italy	73	Saxony . . .	127
France .	74	Bavaria .	132
Belgium .	77	Austria	143

(From Bertillon.)

Births by months. — In table *X* are presented the number of registered births by months in each of five states together with the aggregates for New England. By this table it appears that the greatest number of births occurred in July (10,220) and the next greatest number was in December; the least number occurred in February and the next lowest number was in June.

In order to estimate the actual intensity of the birth-rate at different seasons of the year, the effect of the inequalities in the length of the months has here been eliminated by comparing the births in each month with a daily mean for the whole year and reducing this to a standard mean of 100.

For example, the lower line should read as follows :— For each 100 births which occurred in New England in 1892, in a mean monthly period of uniform length, there were 95.1 births in January, 98.3 in February, etc., in a similar period.

TABLE X.

BIRTHS BY MONTHS—1892.

(Five States.)

Still-births excluded (except in Rhode Island).

	January.	February.	March.	April.	May.	June.	July.	August.	September.	October.	November.	December.	Unknown.	Total.
Maine.........	984 / 84.8	1,088 / 101.2	1,317 / 113.5	1,250 / 111.3	1,297 / 111.8	1,156 / 102.9	1,197 / 103.1	1,168 / 100.7	1,152 / 100.8	1,051 / 88.9	981 / 87.4	1,086 / 93.6	61	13,758
New Hampshire.	591 / 95.5	591 / 102.1	622 / 100.5	616 / 102.8	680 / 111.3	620 / 103.6	626 / 101.1	600 / 96.9	579 / 96.7	586 / 94.7	594 / 99.2	594 / 96.0	19	7,327
Massachusetts...	5,426 / 97.3	5,043 / 96.6	5,438 / 97.5	5,229 / 96.8	5,342 / 95.8	5,129 / 95.1	5,895 / 105.7	5,833 / 104.7	5,500 / 103.6	5,330 / 95.6	5,576 / 103.4	5,980 / 107.4	12	65,824
Rhode Island ...	771 / 98.2	680 / 92.6	782 / 99.6	691 / 90.9	770 / 98.1	718 / 94.5	840 / 107.0	816 / 103.9	796 / 100.8	775 / 98.7	761 / 100.2	900 / 114.6		9,270
Connecticut.....	1,563 / 93.5	1,561 / 103.8	1,668 / 103.7	1,542 / 99.1	1,596 / 99.3	1,471 / 94.5	1,662 / 103.4	1,700 / 105.7	1,550 / 99.6	1,502 / 93.4	1,587 / 102.0	1,440 / 102.0	5	18,987
Five States ...	9,275 / 95.1	8,973 / 98.3	9,824 / 100.7	9,319 / 98.7	9,694 / 99.4	9,004 / 96.3	10,220 / 104.8	10,117 / 103.7	9,617 / 101.9	9,224 / 94.6	9,499 / 100.6	10,210 / 104.7	97	115,166

NOTE.—The same plan is adopted for expressing the seasonal intensity of the birth-rate, as in table VI., p. 17. The second line of figures for each state and for New England is compared with a monthly mean of 100.

DEATHS.

The total number of deaths registered in New England in 1892 was 97,134 and the estimated death-rate per 1,000 of the living population was 19.93.

The highest death-rate (20.6) was that of Massachusetts and the lowest (18.3) was that of Maine.

DEATHS AND DEATH-RATES IN THE NEW ENGLAND STATES, 1892.

States.	Deaths, 1892.	Death-rates per 1,000 inhabitants, 1892.	1891.
Maine	12,147	18.3	——
New Hampshire . .	7,699	20.1	18.7
Vermont	5,960	18.6	16.2
Massachusetts . . .	48,762	20.6	19.6
Rhode Island . . .	7,396	20.3	18.7
Connecticut . . .	15,170	19.6	18.9
New England .	97,134	19.9	19.0

Sex — The deaths of males in New England were 48,922, those of females were 48,140 and the sex of 72 was unknown or not stated.

Estimating the sexes in the living population to have maintained the same ratio as in the census year 1890, namely, males 49.22 per cent. and females 50.78 per cent., or about 1,032 females to 1,000 males, the death-rate of males was 20.3 per 1,000 of living males and those of females was 19.4 per 1,000 of living females, and those of the states were as follows:—

	Males.	Females.
Maine	17.8	18.7
New Hampshire . . .	20.1	20.1
Vermont	17.4	18.4
Massachusetts . . .	21.4	19.8
Rhode Island	21.1	19.7
Connecticut	20.5	18.7
New England . . .	20.4	19 4

TABLE XI.

DEATHS IN 1892— *By Sex and Nativity.*

Exclusive of Still-births.

	Total.	Male.	Female.	Unknown.	NATIVITY.		
					Native.	Foreign.	Unknown.
Maine..........	12,147	5939	6175	33	10,194	1267	686
New Hampshire..........	7099	3811	3880	8	6155	934	890
Vermont..........	5960	2945	2994	21	–	–	–
Massachusetts..........	48,702	24,643	24,119	–	35,097	13,044	621
Rhode Island..........	7396	3725	3671	–	[3216]	[4180]	–
Connecticut..........	15,170	7859	7301	10	11,225	3654	291
	97,134	48,922	48,140	72	62,671	18,899	2497

The figures for Rhode Island in the nativity columns are not included in the totals, since they refer to parent nativity and not to the nativity of the deceased persons.

Deaths by Nativity. — The comments made upon the subject of Nativity under the head of Marriages and Births, apply also to the subject of Deaths.

From the registered deaths in Maine, New Hampshire, Massachusetts and Connecticut (table XI) it appears that 62,671 deaths, or 74.5 per cent., were those of persons of native birth, and, 18,899, or 22.5 per cent., were of persons of foreign birth, and the nativity of 2,497 was unknown.

The highest ratio of deaths of persons of native birth in these four states was in Maine, (83.5) and the lowest (71.8) was in Massachusetts.

Deaths by Ages. — Of the whole number of deaths registered in New England in 1892 (97,345), there were 96,838 whose ages were known. and are stated in Table XII. Of this number, 19,089 were under 1 year of age, or 19.71 per cent.

There were also 8,025 deaths or 8.29 per cent. in the next class or period of life, 1–4 years. The remaining percentages may be found in the table. It is quite manifest, however, that these figures have but very little value, so long as complete census returns of the living population of this district, classified by ages, were not obtainable at the time when this summary was compiled.

The fact, for example, that the deaths in Vermont of infants under 1 year constituted but 16 per cent. of the deaths in that state, while those in Rhode Island constituted 22 per cent., or that the deaths of persons between 80 and 90 years in Vermont were relatively more than double those of Rhode Island for the same period of life, has no significance so long as we are ignorant of the number of persons living at those ages in each state.

Hence, the only accurate conclusion as to the comparative value of the statistics in this table is that which can be made from the figures in the first column (infants under 1), by comparison with the births in the same state, and since the returns of births in Maine and New Hampshire are manifestly defective,

TABLE XII.

Death by Ages — 1892.

States.	Under 1.	1–5.	5–10.	10–20.	20–30.	30–40.	40–50.	50–60.	60–70.	70–80.	80–90.	90–100.	100+	U.	Total.
Maine............	1,706 14.18	672 5.58	262 2.18	582 4.92	973 8.08	751 6.24	777 6.46	1,004 8.34	1,498 12.45	2,033 16.89	1,506 12.50	255 2.12	7 .06	111	12,147
New Hampshire.	1,225 16.33	492 6.65	165 2.18	332 4.40	506 6.70	501 6.63	499 6.61	651 8.76	975 12.91	1,185 15.70	844 11.44	129 1.71	6 .08	149	7,689
Vermont......	981 16.05	325 5.31	168 2.74	271 4.42	407 6.65	377 6.15	376 6.14	457 7.46	780 12.74	1,070 17.47	776 12.67	135 2.20		42	6,165
Massachusetts..	10,649 21.90	4,576 9.41	1,425 2.93	2,140 4.40	4,391 9.03	3,915 8.05	3,704 7.62	4,148 8.53	4,957 10.19	5,116 10.52	3,098 6.37	496 1.02	13 .03	134	48,762
Rhode Island....	1,627 22.04	663 8.98	186 2.52	344 4.66	615 8.33	605 8.19	596 8.07	666 9.02	810 10.97	755 9.96	463 6.27	73 .99		19	7,402
Connecticut.....	2,901 1.92	1,287 8.5	534 3.53	663 4.88	1,236 8.19	1,210 8.00	1,109 7.35	1,339 8.85	1,763 12.50	1,776 11.74	1,129 7.45	222 1.47	9	52	15,170
New England.	19,089 19 71	8,025 8.29	2,740 2.83	4,342 4.49	8,128 8.39	7,359 7.60	7,061 7.29	8,275 8.55	10,723 11.07	11,915 12.30	7,836 8 09	1,310 1.35	55 .04	507	97,345

The percentages are of the total mortality of those whose ages are known.

TABLE XIII.

DEATHS BY MONTHS—1892.

(Five States.)

	January.	February.	March.	April.	May.	June.	July.	August.	September.	October.	November.	December.	Unknown.	Total.
Maine............	1,577 163.9	1,262 134.8	1,005 106.8	1,048 106.7	1,045 102.0	833 84.1	886 84.5	838 91.5	976 98.4	844 82.4	790 79.7	793 77.4	50	12,147
New Hampshire.	1,345 206.7	694 114.0	648 99.6	607 96.4	569 87.4	490 74.5	625 96.1	660 101.4	558 88.6	511 78.5	515 81.8	482 74.1	17	7,699
Massachusetts...	6,399 152.7	3,896 100.8	4,161 100.7	3,990 99.8	3,786 91.6	3,197 80.0	4,565 110.5	4,717 114.1	3,604 91.6	3,484 84.4	3,357 84.0	3,636 88.0	...	48,782
Rhode Island ...	926 147.8	565 101.5	582 92.9	559 92.2	561 89.6	504 83.1	812 129.6	739 118.0	609 100.5	490 78.2	491 81.0	528 84.3		7,393
Connecticut.....	1,986 154.6	1,316 109.5	1,313 102.2	1,150 93.2	1,175 91.4	920 74.7	1,506 117.2	1,440 112.1	1,102 88.6	1,141 88.8	1,037 83.4	1,062 82.7	4	15,170
Five States.....	12,143 157.3	7,703 107.9	7,799 101.0	7,363 98.5	7,136 92.5	5,932 79.4	8,374 108.5	8,404 110.0	6,900 92.5	6,470 83.8	6,190 82.9	6,501 84.2	71	91,174

NOTE.—For explanation of figures in small type see tables VI. and X.

TABLE XIV.

State.	Persons married to 1000 living. Quarter ending				Births to 1000 living. Quarter ending				Deaths to 1000 living. Quarter ending			
	March	June	Sept.	Dec.	March	June	Sept.	Dec.	March	June	Sept.	Dec.
Maine............	11.78	16.73	17.46	22.61	20.49	22.32	21.08	18.67	23.90	17.04	16.76	14.63
New Hampshire.....	17.24	21.35	19.08	26.03	18.85	20.11	18.85	18.53	28.07	17.18	19.25	15.75
Massachusetts......	14.81	20.72	17.79	22.04	26.85	20.40	29.23	28.52	24.25	18.53	21.85	17.08
Rhode Island......	16.87	21.04	17.25	22.40	24.57	23.98	26.65	26.80	23.14	17.87	23.77	16.60
Connecticut.......	—	—	—	—	24.46	23.82	25.39	24.44	23.85	16.86	20.92	16.75
Four states.......	14.68	20.11	17.86	22.95	24.03	24.09	26.30	25.41	24.30	17.04	20.88	16.83
Five states.......												

the comparison can only be correctly made in the remaining states. In these states the ratio of the deaths of infants under 1 to the births was as follows: —

In Vermont, 149.6 per 1,000 births.
In Massachusetts, 161.8 per 1,000 births.
In Rhode Island, 175.5 per 1,000 births.
In Connecticut, 152.8 per 1,000 births.

Seasonal Mortality. — In Table XIII. are presented the statistics of deaths by months in each of the five states for the year 1892. By this table it appears that in each state, as well as in the whole group, the greatest mortality occurred in January (the month in which influenza prevailed to its greatest extent.) The percentage of the yearly mortality in this month was 17.5 in New Hampshire, or nearly double that of any other month of the year.

The lowest mortality, 6.5 per cent. of the yearly deaths, was in June. This month also had the lowest mortality in New Hampshire, Massachusetts, and Connecticut, while the lowest mortality in Maine was in November and December, and in Rhode Island in October and November.

In Table XIV. are presented the birth and death-rates for each quarter and each state except Vermont, and the quarterly marriage rate for each state except Vermont and Connecticut, and for these states collectively.

Causes of Death.

It will be impossible in this summary to state with any degree of accuracy the number of deaths in New England, from unknown, unspecified and ill-defined causes, for the reason that in the different states the deaths embraced in these terms, are variously classified. In some states, for example, the deaths registered as due to heart failure are embraced in this term, in another the deaths from sunstroke, in some the deaths from tumor, hemorrhage, etc., so that it is impossible to state the

number which should be embraced in these terms. It is also
true that indefinite terms like " cephalitis " should be dropped
and replaced by some intelligible names. From this cause one
person is said to have died in Vermont in 1892 and 1,436 in
Massachusetts. No just comparison could, therefore, be made
of statistics relating to diseases of such uncertain and indefinite
nomenclature.

On the other hand, the deaths from specified causes, and
especially those from infectious diseases, are undoubtedly quite
trustworthy and those of one state are comparable with those
of another as well as with those of other countries. For this
reason no attempt is here made to present a complete tabular list
of all diseases, since, in one state, one classification prevails, and
in another state another and more recent classification is in
use. That of Dr. Farr is still in use, where it was first adopted,
while states in which registration is of more recent date, have
made commendable changes. It is quite plain that the rapid
progress of medical science demands a change in the nosology
in use in some of the states.

The plan adopted in this summary is simply that of comparing separately the statistics of the causes of death from certain
diseases which are recognized as preventable, destructive, and
dangerous to the public health, together with certain other
causes which are of public interest and importance, or possibly
have a local, or temporary, character. Most of the infectious
diseases are embraced in the table. The statistics of well-de-
fined diseases of this character may be considered as reasonably
accurate.

In table XV., the figures presented are the number of deaths
in each state in 1892 from each of certain causes, together with
the ratio per 10,000 of the living population of each state. The
totals and means for New England are also given.

Small pox.— There were only 10 registered deaths from small-
pox in New England in 1892. Two of these occurred in Massachusetts, 4 in Rhode Island, and 4 in Connecticut. The death-
rate per 10,000 of the estimated living population of New
England from this cause was .02.

TABLE XV.

CAUSES OF DEATH. — 1892.

Number of Deaths in each State from each of Certain Specified Causes, together with the ratio per 10,000 of the Estimated Population.

Diseases or Causes of Death.	Maine. Deaths.	Maine. Per 10,000 Living.	New Hampshire. D'ths.	New Hampshire. Per 10,000 Living.	Vermont. D'ths.	Vermont. Per 10,000 Living.	Mass. Deaths.	Mass. Per 10,000 Living.	R. I. D'ths.	R. I. Per 10,000 Living.	Connecticut. Deaths.	Connecticut. Per 10,000 Living.	New England. Deaths.	New England. Per 10,000 Living.
Small-pox	—	—	—	—	—	—	2	.01	4	.1	4	.05	10	.02
Measles	29	.4	24	.6	8	.2	88	.4	28	.8	49	.6	226	.5
Scarlet Fever	36	.5	27	.7	43	1.3	669	2.8	67	1.8	280	3.6	1,122	2.3
Diphtheria and Croup	212	3.2	179	4.7	187	5.6	1,455	6.1	178	4.9	542	7.0	2,750	5.6
Typhoid Fever	286	4.3	108	2.8	121	3.6	827	3.5	139	3.8	331	4.3	1,812	3.7
Cholera Infantum	546	8.2	366	9.5	211	6.3	2,898	12.2	632	17.4	968	12.5	5,621	11.5
Phthisis	1,352	20.4	736	19.2	645	19.4	5,739	24.2	809	22.3	1,386	18.3	10,467	21.8
Pneumonia	1,431	21.6	890	23.2	848	25.4	5,020	21.5	655	18.1	1,493	19.3	10,337	21.2
Bronchitis	287	4.3	217	5.7	45	1.3	1,886	7.9	308	8.5	546	7.1	3,287	6.7

Influenza	755	11.4	331	8.6	384	11.5	967	4.1	336	9.2	564	7.3	3,337	0.8
Whooping Cough	54	.8	37	1.0	16	.5	248	1.0	25	.7	64	.8	444	.9
Cerebro Spinal Meningitis	38	.6	19	.5	55	1.6	86	.4	18	.5	40	.6	202	.5
Malarial Fever	13	.2	3	.1	4	.1	81	.3	36	1.0	99	1.3	236	.5
Erysipelas	31	.5	30	1.0	21	.6	234	1.0	25	.7	62	.8	412	.8
Puerperal Fever	42	.6	25	.6	3	.1	81	.3	30	.8	78	1.0	250	.6
Dysentery	48	.7	42	1.3	20	.9	103	.8	71	2.0	105	1.4	488	1.0
Diarrhœa and Cholera Morbus	68	1.0	70	1.8	30	.9	637	2.7	161	4.4	170	2.2	1,136	2.3
Cancer	404	6.1	235	6.1	204	6.1	1,402	5.9	181	5.0	370	4.8	2,706	5.7
Apoplexy and Paralysis	793	12.0	517	12.5	398	12.0	2,880	12.1	362	9.9	704	9.1	5,054	11.6
Insanity	85	1.3	33	.9	11	.3	253	1.1	27	.7	60	.8	469	1.0
All Other Diseases of Nervous System	692	10.4	431	11.2	192	5.8	3,054	12.9	354	9.7	1,100	14.2	5,823	11.9
Diseases of the Circulatory Organs	895	13.5	611	15.9	614	18.5	4,150	17.5	500	14.0	1,125	14.5	7,900	16.2
Diseases of the Kidneys	265	4.0	222	5.8	149	4.5	1,509	6.6	258	7.1	482	6.2	2,945	6.0
Accident	376	5.7	229	6.0	150	4.5	1,819	7.6	300	8.5	587	7.6	3,020	7.4
Suicide	59	.9	51	1.3	24	.7	274	1.2	19	.5	93	1.2	520	1.1
Old Age	780	11.8	441	11.5	399	12.0	1,895	8.0	256	7.0	643	8.3	4,414	9.0

Measles. — The deaths from measles were 226, or .46 per 10,000 of the living population of New England. The highest death-rate from this cause (.77) was in Rhode Island, and the lowest (.24) in Vermont.

Scarlet Fever. — The deaths from scarlet fever in New England were 1,122 and the death-rate 2.3 per 10,000. The highest death-rate from this cause (3.6) occurred in Connecticut, and the lowest (.54) in Maine.

Diphtheria and Croup. — In accordance with common modern usage, diphtheria and fatal croup are grouped together. From these causes there were 2,750 deaths in New England and the death-rate was 5.6. The highest rate (7.0) was in Connecticut, and the lowest (3.2) was in Maine.

Typhoid Fever. — From this cause there were 1,812 deaths in New England in 1892, and the death-rate was 3.7. The highest death-rate from this cause was in Maine (4.3) and the lowest (2.8) was in New Hampshire.

Whooping-cough. — The deaths from this cause in New England were 444 and the death-rate was .91. The highest death-rate from this cause (1.05) was in Massachusetts, and the lowest (.48) was in Vermont.

Cerebro-Spinal Meningitis. — The deaths from this cause in New England were 262, and the death-rate .53. The highest death-rate from the same cause was 1.65 in Vermont, and the lowest (.36) in Massachusetts.

Erysipelas. — The deaths from erysipelas in New England were 412, and the death-rate was .84. The highest death-rate from the same cause (1.02) was in New Hampshire, and the lowest (.47) was in Maine.

Puerperal Fever. — From this cause 259 deaths were registered in 1892 in New England, and the death-rate from the same cause was .59. The highest death-rate (1.01) was in Connecticut, and the lowest (.09) was in Vermont.

Influenza. — The whole number of registered deaths from influenza in New England in 1892 was 3337, and the death-rate was 6.8 per 10,000 of the living population. The highest death-rate from this cause (11.5) was in Vermont, and the lowest (4.08) was in Massachusetts. The number of deaths from this cause in January and February was 2469, or more than 74 per cent. of the whole number. The measure of the incidence of this disease upon the population is not alone found in the deaths registered under this term "influenza," but also to a considerable extent in the increase of deaths from pneumonia, bronchitis, consumption, heart disease, old age, and a few other causes.

Consumption.—The total number of deaths from this most destructive disease was 10,667, and the death-rate 21.8. The highest death-rate from this cause (24.2) was in Massachusetts, and the lowest (18.3) was in Connecticut. In those states which have had registration for several years, the mortality from this cause is found to be steadily diminishing.

Pneumonia.—The total number of deaths from pneumonia in New England in 1892 was 10,337, and the death-rate from the same cause was 21.2. The highest death-rate (25.4) was in Vermont, and the lowest (18.1) was in Rhode Island

In the sea-coast districts the pneumonia death-rate is generally lower than that of the inland or elevated regions. The death-rate of Franklin and Caledonia counties in Vermont from this cause was 23.2 in 1892, and that of Bennington county in the same state was only 17.0. In Massachusetts, for the 20-year period 1871–1890, the pneumonia death-rate of the four western or inland counties was as follows:

Berkshire,	16.6	Hampshire,	15.9
Franklin,	16.4	Hampden,	16.3

and those of the southeastern counties were as follows:

Nantucket,	9.7	Plymouth,	11.6
Dukes,	10.8	Barnstable,	11.6

Bronchitis.—The total deaths from bronchitis were 3287, and the death-rate was 6.7. The highest death-rate from this cause was in Rhode Island (8 5), and the lowest was in Vermont (1.3).

A better measure of the mortality from acute lung disease may be had by taking the sum of these three causes—pneumonia, bronchitis and influenza — by which it appears that the combined death-rate from these three causes was more uniform throughout the six states than that of either cause considered by itself. The total deaths from these causes were 10,961, and the death-rate was 34.7. That of the states was as follows:

Maine,	37.3	Massachusetts,	33 5
New Hampshire,	37.5	Rhode Island,	35.8
Vermont,	38.3	Connecticut,	33.7

Dysentery. — The deaths from dysentery in New England in 1892 were 488 and the death-rate 1 per 10,000 of the population. The highest mortality for this cause (1.9), was in Rhode Island and the lowest was in Maine (.7).

Diarrhœa and Cholera Morbus.— The deaths from these causes were 1,136 and the death-rate 2.32. The highest death-rate was 4.4 in Rhode Island and the lowest .9 in Vermont.

Cholera Infantum.— Under this term are included the deaths registered from cholera infantum and from infantile diarrhœa, — 5,621 in number. The death-rate from this cause in New England was 11.5. The highest was 17.4 in Rhode Island and the lowest (6.3), was in Vermont.

The total deaths from the foregoing diarrhœal diseases in New England in 1892 were 7,245, and the combined death-rate, 14.82. Those of the six states from these combined causes were as follows :

Maine,	10.0	Massachusetts,	15.7
New Hampshire,	12.6	Rhode Island,	23.7
Vermont,	8.1	Connecticut,	16.1

*Malarial Fever.**— The total deaths from malarial fever in New England were 236, and the death-rate from this cause was .48. The highest death-rate was 1.28 in Connecticut, and the lowest (.03), was in New Hampshire. Malarial fever can scarcely be said to exist in the three northern states of New England.

NOTE.— An eminent New England physician has very aptly described malarial fever in New England as a "tender exotic," which requires peculiar climatic conditions for its continuance. In nearly every instance where the disease has prevailed in New England, it has disappeared in a few years after its first appearance.

Diseases of the Nervous System.

Apoplexy and Paralysis. — The number of deaths registered under these two headings in New England in 1892 was 5,654, and the death-rate per 10,000 of the population was 11.57. The highest death-rate from the same causes was 13.5 in New Hampshire, and the lowest (9.1) was in Connecticut.

Insanity. — The number of deaths charged to insanity in New England was 496, and the death-rate was .96. The highest death-rate from this cause (1.28) was in Maine, and the lowest (.33) was in Vermont.

All Other Diseases of the Nervous System. — From all other diseases of the nervous system there were 5,823 deaths, or 11.92 per 10,000 of the population. The highest death-rate from these causes was 14.2 in Connecticut and the lowest (5.8) was in Vermont.

From the three foregoing causes combined there were 11,946 deaths, and the combined death-rate was 24.45.

Cancer. — The number of deaths attributed to Cancer in New England in 1892 was 2,796, and the death-rate was 5.7 per 10,000 of the population. The highest death-rate from this cause was in Vermont (6.14), and the lowest was in Connecticut (4.77). These differences are probably due to the existence of a greater ratio of persons above 50 years of age in the three northern states of the district as compared with the three southern states (Massachusetts, Rhode Island and Connecticut).

Diseases of the Circulatory System. — The total number of deaths attributed to diseases of the circulatory organs was 7,900, and the death-rate per 10,000 was 16.17. The highest (18.5) was in Vermont, and the lowest was in Maine (13.5).

Kidney Diseases. — The whole number of deaths ascribed to kidney diseases in New England was 2,945, and the death-rate was 6.02 per 10,000 of the population. The highest death-rate from this cause (7.09) was in Rhode Island, and the lowest (4.00) was in Maine.

Accident. — The deaths from accident in New England were
3,620, and the death-rate was 7.4. The highest death-rate
from this cause, or group of causes, was 8 5 in Rhode Island,
and the lowest was 4.5 in Vermont.

Suicide. — There were 520 registered deaths from suicide,
and the death-rate from this cause was 1.06. The death-rates
ranged from a maximum of 1.33 in New Hampshire to a
minimum of .52 in Rhode Island.

Old Age. — The fact that there were 4,414 deaths recorded
under the title of old age has but little significance, and the
greater death-rate of the three northern states under this term,
as was stated under the title " Cancer," simply means that the
number of old persons was relatively greater in these states.

The following infectious diseases have characteristics of
peculiar interest to the sanitarian, and yet their incidence upon
the New England population in 1892 was comparatively
insignificant.

Hydrophobia was unusually prevalent in 1888, 1889 and
1890, but in 1892 only two deaths from this cause, were registered one in Massachusetts and one in Connecticut.

There were no reported deaths from *glanders*, *trichinosis* or
Asiatic cholera in 1892.

Anthrax or *malignant pustule* finds an occasional victim in
towns in which foreign hides and other animal products are
treated. There were six deaths from this cause reported in
1892, five of which were in Massachusetts and one in Rhode
Island.

Vital Statistics of Cities.

The rapid increase of the urban population in New England
gives to the vital statistics of the cities a special interest. In
the following table (table, XVI.), in which are presented the
vital statistics of all cities and towns having more than 10,000
inhabitants in each, the figures may be regarded as reasonably
correct, with the exception of the registered births in some of

the cities of Maine and New Hampshire, which are probably deficient in number.

The items presented are the population of each city by the census of 1890, the number of registered marriages, births and deaths in each in 1892, the general death-rate per 1,000 for the same year, using for this purpose the estimated population for 1892, and the number of deaths and death-rates per 10,000 from eight selected causes of death, which are of special interest to the sanitarian.

The estimates of population for all places having over 20,000 inhabitants are made by the geometric rate of increase during the last census interval, and those of all of the smaller cities by the arithmetric rate.

From this table it appears that the total number of marriages in these towns registered in 1892 was 25,223, and the marriage-rate was 10.33 (persons married 20.66).

The total number of births registered was 72,456 and the birth-rate was 29.68.

The total number of deaths was 51,375, and the death-rate was 21.01.

The following are the maximum and minimum death-rates in the foregoing list:—

DEATHS PER 1,000 OF THE LIVING POPULATION.

Biddeford .	27.6	Auburn	. . .	15.7
Lowell	26.6	Waltham	. . .	15.7
Lawrence	26.4	Lewiston		15.2
Chicopee	26.2	Quincy	.	15.1
Dover	25.4	Hyde Park .	. .	15.0
Fall River .	24.0	Peabody	. . .	15.0
Concord	23.5	Newton	. . .	14.8
Holyoke .	23.4	Brookline	. . .	14.8
Boston	23.3	Clinton	. .	14.5
Hartford,	. 22.9	Brockton	. . .	13.7

From certain special causes the maximum and minimum death-rates were as follows : —

TABLE XVI.

Vital Statistics of New England Cities and Towns having

Arranged according to number of

Number.	City and State.	Population, 1890.	Marriages.	Births.	Deaths.	Death Rate, 1892, per 1,000 Population.	Deaths from Scarlet Fever.	Death Rate from Scarlet Fever.	Deaths from Diphtheria and Croup.	Death Rate from Diphtheria and Croup.
1	Boston, Mass.,	448,477	5,315	15,466	11,221	23.3	261	5.5	485	10.2
2	Providence, R. I.,	132,146	1,582	3,953	2,964	21.4	38	2.7	72	5.2
3	Worcester, Mass.,	84,655	878	2,853	1,817	19.6	15	1.6	69	7.5
4	New Haven, Conn.,	81,298	918	2,581	1,779	19.5	44	4.8	84	9.2
5	Lowell, Mass.,	77,696	948	2,731	2,229	26.6	13	1.5	28	3.3
6	Fall River, Mass.,	74,398	872	2,596	1,986	24.0	27	3.3	59	7.1
7	Cambridge, Mass.,	70,028	733	2,338	1,523	20.4	16	2.1	53	7.1
8	Lynn, Mass.,	55,727	657	1,653	1,086	18.0	3	.5	30	5.0
9	Hartford, Conn.,	53,230	633	1,401	1,277	22.9	31	5.5	103	18.5
10	Bridgeport, Conn.,	48,866	570	1,699	955	17 4	18	3.3	22	4.0
11	Lawrence, Mass.,	44,654	538	1,311	1,246	26.4	44	9.3	28	5.9
12	Springfield, Mass.,	44,179	469	1,395	995	21.2	14	3.0	48	10.2
13	Manchester, N. H.,	44,126	739	1,029	1,038	22.2	2	.4	11	2.3
14	New Bedford, Mass.,	40,733	515	1,659	991	22.5	4	.9	10	2.3
15	Somerville, Mass.,	40,152	426	1,282	718	15.9	13	2.9	8	1.8
16	Portland, Me.,	36,425	207	808	782	21.2	3	.8	12	3.2
17	Holyoke, Mass.,	35,637	413	1,646	922	23.4	13	3.3	71	18.1
18	Salem, Mass.,	30,801	293	880	717	22.5	3	.9	11	3.4
19	Waterbury, Conn.,	28,646	291	1,210	710	19.4	7	1.9	20	5.5
20	Chelsea, Mass.,	27,909	342	918	650	22.5	13	4.5	18	6.2
21	Pawtucket, R. I,	27,633	331	726	642	21.6	5	1.7	9	3.0
22	Haverhill, Mass.,	27,412	314	781	495	16.5	5	1.7	2	.7
23	Brockton, Mass.,	27,294	270	711	416	13.7	2	.7	15	4.9
24	Taunton, Mass.,	25,448	232	714	505	22.7	8	3.0	12	4.6
25	Gloucester, Mass.,	24,651	223	652	431	16.6	4	1.5	2	.8
26	Newton, Mass.,	24,379	247	639	393	14.8	–	–	8	3.0
43	Norwich, Conn.,	23,048	222	584	455	19.4	9	3.8	6	2.6
27	Malden, Mass,	23,031	244	787	452	17.1	7	2.6	13	4.9
28	Fitchburg, Mass.,	22,037	203	909	445	17.5	2	.8	6	2.4
29	Lewiston, Me	21,701	250	535	340	15.2	–	–	9	4.0
30	Meriden, Conn.,	21,652	244	834	455	17.0	1	.4	13	4.8
31	Woonsocket, R. I.,	20,830	220	713	445	19.3	6	2.6	8	3.5
32	Lincoln, R. I.	20,355	170	701	450	20.7	2	.9	4	1.8
33	Newport, R. I	19,467	151	488	404	20.8	4	2.0	27	13.9
34	Nashua, N H.,	19,311	266	698	402	19.6	–	–	3	1.5
35	Bangor, Me.,	19,103	211	365	364	18.3	–	–	–	–
36	Waltham, Mass.,	18,767	219	575	319	15.7	10	4.9	–	–
37	Warwick, R. I.,	17,761	171	480	381	19.1	2	1.0	8	4.0
38	Norwalk, Conn.,	17,747	155	431	336	18.3	2	1.1	15	8.1
39	Pittsfield, Mass.,	17,281	128	502	322	17.5	10	5.4	12	6.5
40	Concord, N. H.,	17,004	176	416	415	23.5	3	1.7	3	1.7
41	Quincy, Mass.,	16,723	148	613	288	15.1	2	1.1	10	5.4
42	New Britain, Conn.,	16,519	218	644	353	17.6	3	1.5	17	8.5
44	North Adams, Mass.,	16,074	154	602	345	19.7	8	4.6	34	19.5
45	Stamford, Conn.,	15,700	94	495	378	22.8	29	17.5	28	16.8
46	Northampton, Mass.,	14,990	128	366	267	16.8	6	3.8	9	5.7
47	Burlington, Vt.,	14,590	150	396	338	22.2	4	2.6	3	2.0
48	Biddeford, Me.,	14,443	151	509	408	27.6	–	–	20	13.5
49	Chicopee, Mass.,	14,050	232	567	305	20.2	7	4.6	5	3.3
50	Newburyport, Mass.,	13,947	113	338	310	22.2	4	2.8	23	16.4
51	Marlboro, Mass	13,805	116	444	241	16.1	3	2.0	3	2.0
52	New London, Conn.,	13,757	154	369	287	19.9	6	4.2	2	1.4
53	Woburn, Mass.,	13,499	95	419	270	19.0	4	2.8	8	5.6
54	Dover, N. H.,	12,790	105	296	331	25.4	2	1.5	10	7.7
55	Brookline, Mass.,	12,103	143	364	196	14.8	–	–	4	3.0
56	Rutland, Vt.,	11,760	104	264	209	16.6	–	–	19	15.1
57	Auburn, Me.,	11,250	103	151	182	15.7	3	2.6	5	4.3
58	Medford, Mass.,	11,079	85	330	207	17.4	3	2.5	3	2.5
59	Everett, Mass.,	11,068	123	511	255	19.4	3	2.3	10	7.6
60	Weymouth, Mass.,	10,866	80	234	200	18.3	2	1.8	4	3.7
61	Beverly, Mass.,	10,821	78	248	206	18.0	–	–	1	.9
62	Augusta, Me.,	10,527	151	206	222	20.4	–	1.0	7	6.4
63	Clinton, Mass.,	10,424	122	342	160	14.5	2	.8	2	1.8
64	Ansonia, Conn	10,342	89	374	185	16.8	1	.9	4	3.6
65	Hyde Park, Mass.,	10,193	81	280	164	15.0	–	–	3	2.8
66	Peabody, Mass.,	10,158	56	219	156	15.0	1	1.0	–	–
67	Greenwich, Conn.,	10,131	55	214	177	16.7	1	.9	1	.9
–	All the Cities,	–	25,223	72,456	51,203	21.0	768	3.1	1,552	6.3

Population by Census of 1890.

RATES FROM CERTAIN CAUSES, PER 10,000 LIVING.

Deaths from Typhoid Fever.	Death Rate from Typhoid Fever.	Deaths from Cholera Infantum.	Death Rate from Cholera Infantum.	Deaths from Phthisis.	Death Rate from Phthisis.	Deaths from Pneumonia.	Death Rate from Pneumonia.	Deaths from Bronchitis.	Death Rate from Bronchitis.	Number.
137	2.9	563	11.9	1,552	32.8	1,144	24.2	543	11.5	1
52	3.8	201	14.5	371	26.8	277	20.0	130	9.4	2
17	1.8	127	13.9	207	22.5	158	17.3	84	9.1	3
28	2.9	142	15.6	168	18.5	146	16.0	104	11.4	4
77	9.2	229	27.3	231	27.6	215	25.7	114	13.6	5
27	3.3	228	27.5	163	19.7	175	21.2	101	12.2	6
15	2.0	92	13.3	216	28.9	132	17.7	74	9.9	7
13	2.2	74	12.3	134	22.2	136	22.6	28	4.6	8
46	8.2	53	9.5	129	23.2	117	21.0	45	8.0	9
7	1.3	61	11.1	93	17.0	98	17.9	29	5.3	10
50	10.6	130	27.6	95	20.1	156	33.1	27	5.7	11
39	8.3	63	13.4	116	24.6	76	16.1	48	10.2	12
5	1.1	102	21.8	91	19.4	50	10.7	38	8.1	13
15	3.4	72	16.3	125	28.3	84	19.0	29	6.6	14
14	3.1	38	8.4	90	19.9	68	15.1	32	7.1	15
6	1.6	29	7.8	80	21.7	107	29.0	20	5.4	16
16	4.1	72	18.3	88	22.4	102	26.0	30	7.6	17
18	5.6	46	14.4	77	24.2	78	24.5	32	10.0	18
29	8.0	75	20.5	80	21.9	65	17.8	31	8.5	19
10	3.5	34	11.8	83	28.7	71	24.6	21	7.2	20
15	5.0	71	23.8	54	18.2	41	13.8	46	15.4	21
13	4.3	26	8.6	80	26.6	44	14.6	16	5.3	22
8	2.6	16	5.2	49	16.1	52	17.1	11	3.6	23
9	3.4	30	11.5	61	23.3	67	25.6	24	9.2	24
3	1.1	16	6.1	50	19.3	48	18.5	11	4.2	25
4	1.5	17	6.4	46	17.4	46	17.4	19	7.1	26
4	1.7	38	16.2	51	21.8	44	18.8	6	2.6	27
6	2.3	23	8.7	52	19.7	29	11.0	7	2.7	28
-	-	40	15.7	43	16.9	54	21.2	19	7.4	29
36	16.2	47	21.1	30	13.5	32	14.4	11	4.9	30
10	3.7	47	17.5	49	18.3	34	12.7	10	3.7	31
8	3.5	50	21.7	52	22.6	48	20.8	13	5.6	32
10	4.5	81	37.1	51	23.5	29	13.7	28	12.9	33
5	2.6	31	16.0	35	18.0	37	19.0	19	9.8	34
7	3.4	36	17.5	26	12.7	55	26.8	22	10.7	35
21	10.7	14	7.1	56	28.5	40	20.4	11	5.6	36
5	2.5	7	3.4	59	29.0	46	22.6	15	7.4	37
6	3.0	64	32.1	32	16.1	34	17.1	7	3.5	38
6	3.2	19	10.3	27	14.6	30	16.2	18	9.7	39
6	3.3	9	4.9	37	20.1	51	27.7	13	7.0	40
2	1.1	20	11.3	35	19.8	44	23.0	7	3.9	41
7	3.8	11	5.9	51	27.5	17	9.1	6	3.2	42
9	4.5	29	14.5	27	13.5	39	19.5	20	10.0	43
11	6.3	26	14.9	41	23.4	41	23.4	5	2.8	44
5	3.0	14	8.4	26	15.7	52	31.4	8	4.8	45
3	1.9	20	12.6	27	17.1	28	17.7	13	8.2	46
3	2.0	37	24.3	41	26.9	17	11.1	3	2.0	47
18	12.2	53	35.8	40	27.0	53	35.8	9	6.1	48
24	15.9	36	23.9	41	27.2	39	25.9	20	13.3	49
3	2.1	14	10.0	42	29.9	23	16.3	13	9.2	50
3	2.0	17	11.3	30	20.0	30	20.0	5	3.3	51
9	6.3	23	15.9	29	20.1	19	13.2	6	4.2	52
8	5.6	12	8.4	35	24.6	25	17.6	9	6.3	53
5	3.8	18	13.8	37	28.4	30	23.0	5	3.8	54
1	.8	10	7.5	19	14.3	21	15.8	9	6.8	55
2	1.6	21	16.7	25	19.9	25	19.9	1	.8	56
3	2.6	10	8.6	16	13.8	22	19.0	2	1.7	57
2	1.7	15	12.6	18	15.1	14	11.8	8	6.7	58
1	.8	19	14.4	30	22.8	28	21.2	8	6.1	59
4	3.7	8	7.3	20	18.3	17	15.6	14	12.8	60
3	2.6	6	5.2	27	23.6	18	15.7	11	9.6	61
9	8.3	26	23.8	35	32.1	32	29.4	11	10.1	62
1	.9	23	20.9	13	11.8	12	10.9	10	9.1	63
8	7.2	17	15.5	20	18.2	13	11.8	17	15.5	64
3	2.8	6	5.5	24	22.0	22	20.2	7	6.4	65
4	3.8	11	10.5	15	14.4	17	16.3	4	3.8	66
3	2.8	15	14.2	15	14.2	5	4.7	7	6.6	67
985	3.9	3,690	14.9	5,008	24.2	5,010	20.5	2,124	8.7	-

From *Measles*.   Deaths per 10,000 of the living population.

The deaths from *Measles* were omitted from the foregoing table for economy of space.   In forty-two cities, no deaths from this cause were registered in 1892.   Those in the remaining cities were as follows:—Boston, 34; Manchester, 18; New Haven, 12; Providence, 11; Lowell, 11; Woonsocket, 10; Fall River, 8; Holyoke, 8; Auburn, 5; Springfield, 3; Cambridge, Portland, Newport and Warwick, 2 each; and Worcester, Lynn, Hartford, Bridgeport, Lawrence, Waterbury, Brockton, Newton, Quincy, New Britain and Chicopee, 1 each. The highest death-rates from this cause were those of Woonsocket, 4.3; Auburn, 4.3; Manchester, 3.8; Holyoke, 2.0; and New Haven, 1.3; per 10,000 living.

From *Scarlet-fever*.   The maximum death-rates from scarlet-fever were as follows:—

Stamford, 17.5; Lawrence, 9.3; Hartford, 5.5; Boston, 5.5; Pittsfield, 5.4; Waltham, 4.9; Chicopee, 4.6; Chelsea, 4.5; and there were no deaths from scarlet-fever in the following cities:—

Newton, Brookline, Rutland, Lewiston, Beverly, Nashua, Augusta, Bangor, Biddeford, Hyde Park.

From *Diphtheria and Croup*.   The maximum and minimum death-rates from diphtheria and croup were as follows:—

North Adams	19.5	Nashua	1.5
Hartford	18.5	New London	1.4
Holyoke	18.1	Beverly	.9
Stamford	16.8	Greenwich	.9
Newburyport	16.4	Gloucester	.8
Rutland	15.1	Haverhill	.7
Newport	13.9	Lynn	.5
Biddeford	13.5	Bangor	0
Boston	10.2	Waltham	0
Springfield	10.2	Peabody	0

Typhoid Fever. The maximum and death-rates from typhoid-fever were as follows : —

DEATH-RATES PER 10,000.

Lewiston	16.2	Portland		1.6+
Chicopee	15.9	Rutland		1.6—
Biddeford	12.2	Newton		1.5
Bangor	10.7	Bridgeport		1.3
Lawrence	10.6	Gloucester		1.15
Lowell	9.1	Concord		1.1
Springfield	8.3	Manchester		1.07
Augusta	8.3	Clinton		.9
Hartford	8.2	Brookline		.8
Waterbury	8.0	Everett		.8

Cholera Infantum. The maximum and minimum death-rates from cholera infantum were as follows : —

Lincoln	37.1	Brookline		7.5
Biddeford	35.8	Weymouth		7.3
Warwick	32.1	Bangor		7.1
Lawrence	27.6	Newton		6.4
Fall River	27.5	Gloucester		6.1
Lowell	27.3	Hyde Park		5.5
Burlington	24.3	Brockton		5.2
Chicopee	23.9	Beverly		5.2
Augusta	23.8	Pittsfield		4.9
Pawtucket	23.8	Waltham		3.4

Phthisis. From consumption the maximum and minimum death-rates were as follows : —

Boston	32.8	Medford	15.1
Augusta	32.1	Norwalk	14.6
Newburyport	29.9	Peabody	14.4
Waltham	29.0	Brookline	14.3
Cambridge	28.9	Greenwich	14.2
Chelsea	28.7	Auburn	13.8
Bangor	28.5	New Britain	13.5
Dover	28.4	Lewiston	13.5
New Bedford	28.3	Nashua	12.7
Lowell	27.6	Clinton	11.8

It is worthy of notice that all of the following cities lying on or quite near the southern sea-coast of New England had death-rates from Phthisis considerably below the mean : — Fall River, Newport, Warwick, New London, New Haven, Bridgeport, Stamford, Norwalk, Greenwich.

Pneumonia. The maximum and minimum death-rates from pneumonia were as follows : —

Biddeford	. . .	35.8	Pawtucket	13.8
Lawrence	. .	33.1	Lincoln .	13.7
Stamford	. . .	31.4	New London .	13.2
Augusta	. . .	29.4	Ansonia . .	11.8+
Portland	.	29.0	Medford .	11.8—
Pittsfield	. . .	27.7	Burlington	11.1
Nashua	. .	26.8	Malden . .	11.0
Holyoke	. .	26.0	Clinton . .	10.9
Chicopee	. . .	25.9	Manchester .	10.7
Lowell	. . .	25.7	Quincy . .	9.1

Bronchitis. The maximum and minimum death-rates from bronchitis were as follows : —

Ansonia	. .	15.5	Brockton .	. 3.6
Pawtucket	. .	15.4	Warwick .	. 3.5
Lowell	. .	13.6	Marlboro' . .	. 3.3
Chicopee	. .	13.3	Quincy . .	. 3.2
Lincoln	. .	12.9	North Adams	2.8
Weymouth	. .	12.8	Malden .	2.7
Fall River .	. .	12.2	Norwich .	. 2.6
Boston	. .	11.5	Burlington .	. 2.0
New Haven	. .	11.4	Auburn . .	. 1.7
Nashua	. .	10.7	Rutland . .	.8

The following figures present the combined death-rates from these three diseases — phthisis, pneumonia and bronchitis — in those cities which had the highest and lowest mortality from these causes in 1892 : —

Phthisis, Pneumonia and Bronchitis.

DEATHS PER 10,000 POPULATION.

Augusta	71.6		Brockton	.	36.8
Biddeford	. . 68.9		Warwick	.	. 36.7
Boston	68.5		Peabody	. .	. 34.6
Lowell	66.9		Auburn	. .	. 34.5
Chicopee	66.4		Medford	.	. 33.6
Chelsea	60.5		Malden	. .	. 33.4
Waltham	. . 59.0		Lewiston	.	. 32.8
Salem .	. . . 58.7		Clinton	. .	. 31.8
Taunton	. . . 58.1		Greenwich .	.	. 25.5

The death-rates of each of the remaining cities from the fore-going causes may be found in table XVI.

Interesting results are obtained by grouping the cities in this table according to their populations.

While such a classification cannot be considered as an exact division of the cities according to the density of their populations, it may be taken as an approximate grouping of this nature.

Four groups are made, the first embracing the two cities having more than 100,000 inhabitants in each. Boston and Providence, with a total estimated population in 1892 of 612,298.

The second group includes those cities having more than 50,000, but less than 100,000 in each, the total estimated population being 535,238.

The third group includes those cities having more than 25,000, but less than 50,000 in each, with a total estimated population of 570,230.

The fourth group embraces the remaining cities and towns having more than 10,000, but less than 25,000, in each, with a total estimated population of 723,652 in 1892.

This general division of the whole district may fairly be compared with the remainder of the district comprising a nearly equal population, the estimated population of the urban population in 1892 being 2,441,418, and that of the rural population being 2,444,987.

The marriage, birth and death-rates of these two principal groups of population were as follows for 1892, still bearing in mind the probable deficiency of birth registration in Maine and New Hampshire : —

	Marriage-rates.	Birth-rates.	Death-rates.
Urban Group............	20.66	29.68	21.01
Rural Group...	16.42	20.00	18.72

Reducing these figures to a standard of 1,000 for the total population the rank of these populations would stand as follows : —

	Married Persons.	Births.	Deaths.
Urban Group............	1114	1195	1058
New England........	**1000**	**1000**	**1000**
Rural Group......	886	805	943

The foregoing may be read as follows : —

For each 1,000 persons married in New England as a whole, there were in equal numbers living in the urban population, 1,114 persons married, and in the rural population 886, &c.

For the diseases mentioned in table XVI. a similar method of presentation gives the following results, in this case the number 100 for New England as a whole being taken as the standard of comparison. In this grouping the cities are presented in four divisions, as already suggested : —

General Mortality and Mortality from Eight Diseases by Groups.

Groups.	General Mortality.	Measles.	Scarlet Fever.	Diphtheria and Croup.	Typhoid Fever	Cholera Infantus.	Consumption.	Pneumonia.	Bronchitis.
Cities having over 100,000 populations in each	116	158	213	162	84	110	144	109	164
Cities having from 50,000 to 100,000	110	146	122	142	112	154	107	95	153
Cities having from 25,000 to 50,000	105	133	117	43	122	132	101	96	113
Cities having from 10,000 to 25,000	95	70	91	62	109	138	94	90	97
The Whole Urban Group.	106	126	135	121	105	133	111	97	129
New England	100	100	100	100	100	100	100	100	100
The Rural Group	94	79	65	80	95	68	89	102	70

The foregoing table may be read as follows : — For each 100 persons who died in the whole district of New England in 1892 from all causes, 106 died in the cities and large towns and 94 in the rural districts ; 116 in the large cities, 110 in those of the second group, 105 in those of the third group and 95 in those of the fourth group.

For each 100 who died of measles in the whole district, 126 died from the same cause in the cities and large towns, and 79 in the rural districts: 158 died in the large cities, 146 in those of the second group, 133 in those of the third and 70 in those of the fourth, &c.

The following additional statistics relative to births are to be found in the reports of New Hampshire, Rhode Island and Connecticut: —

NUMBER OF THE CHILDREN OF THE MOTHER, 1892.

	N. H.	R. I.	R. I., 36 years.	Conn.	Conn., 10 years.
1st . .	2,266	2,383	53,260	5,833	44,649
2d . .	1,523	1,754	42,983	3,959	34,498
3d . .	1,010	1,444	33,361	3,011	24,578
4th . .	691	1,050	25,143	2,176	17,641
5th . .	477	754	18,787	1,525	12,426
6th . .	399	520	13,786	1,088	9,075
7th .	252	416	9,869	724	6,469
8th . .	185	311	7,074	481	4,522
9th .	106	218	4,750	364	3,162
10th .	83	149	3,198	245	2,023
11th . .	60	113	1,918	152	1,185
12th .	46	75	1,219	88	778
13th .	33	36	680	67	498
14th .	21	18	343	29	244
15th .	6	13	190	14	132
16th .	7	10	92	9	64
17th . .	3	4	56	3	28
18th .	3	1	25	1	11
19th .	2	1	13	–	6
20th .	1	–	6	1	4
21st .	–	–	3	–	12
22d .	–	–	2	–	1
23d . .	–	–	–	–	1

In the reports of Connecticut this table is classified into children of native and foreign parentage.

Among native parents the firstlings constituted 31.2 per cent. of the whole number of children, and among foreign parents they were 22.4 per cent. of the whole. The ratio of children who were the fifth, sixth, and upwards among foreign parents was much greater than it was among natives.

Meteorology.

The following table is taken from the bulletin of the New England Meteorological Society for 1892. It consists of the means of the observations of about 150 voluntary observers distributed throughout New England, with a reasonable degree of uniformity. The barometric observations are by twenty observers only : —

NEW ENGLAND WEATHER.

Months.	Mean Atmospheric Pressure. In Inches.	Mean Temperature. In Degrees F.	Departure from Normal.	Precipitation in Inches.	Departure from Normal.
January..............	30.00	24.6	+2.0	4.81	+0.88
February	30.12	25.9	+1.8	2.09	—1.64
March....	29.91	29.7	—1.3	3.20	—0.75
April..............	30.00	44.8	+1.3	1.02	—2.13
May.....	29.97	53.6	—1.4	5.23	+1.79
June........	29.96	68.1	+1.7	3.92	+0.42
July................	30.02	70.0	+0.6	2.91	—1.03
August...	30.01	67.8	+0.1	5.45	+1.22
September..........	30.13	58.5	—0.7	2.24	—1.17
October.... ....|	29.93	44.6	—0.3	1.50	—2.38
November...	30.04	37.7	—0.3	5.10	+1.19
December..........	29.98	24.9	—2.2	1.32	—2.15
Mean..............	30.01	45.85	+0.2		—0.18
Total...........				39.79